YOUR KNOWLEDGE HAS VALUE

Janina Bohling

Outsourcing and Third Party Logistics

GRIN Verlag

Bibliografische Information der Deutschen Nationalbibliothek:

Die Deutsche Bibliothek verzeichnet diese Publikation in der Deutschen National-
bibliografie; detaillierte bibliografische Daten sind im Internet über http://dnb.d-
nb.de/ abrufbar.

Imprint:

Copyright © 2013 GRIN Verlag GmbH
Druck und Bindung: Books on Demand GmbH, Norderstedt Germany
ISBN: 978-3-656-54748-8

This book at GRIN:

http://www.grin.com/en/e-book/265030/outsourcing-and-third-party-logistics

GRIN - Your knowledge has value

Der GRIN Verlag publiziert seit 1998 wissenschaftliche Arbeiten von Studenten, Hochschullehrern und anderen Akademikern als eBook und gedrucktes Buch. Die Verlagswebsite www.grin.com ist die ideale Plattform zur Veröffentlichung von Hausarbeiten, Abschlussarbeiten, wissenschaftlichen Aufsätzen, Dissertationen und Fachbüchern.

Heriot-Watt University

School of Management and Languages

MSc Logistics and Supply Chain Management

Outsourcing and Third Party Logistics

Critically evaluate the development of third party logistics companies (3PLs) from the initial outsourcing of warehousing to their partnership in supply chain activities today.

Module Title	Strategy for Supply Chains
Module Code	C11LS
Name	Janina Bohling
Word Count	2,199 (main text, excl. reference list, figures, headings)

Table of Content

List of figures

Introduction

The process of globalization and the removal of barriers to international trade have led to an increased importance of Supply Chain Management for most businesses involved. To remain competitive, there is a need for all partners within the supply chain to collaborate and communicate (Zacharia et al. 2011; Christopher 2011). These two requirements, together with the creation of efficiency in all processes involved, an increased concentration on core competencies and the outsourcing of certain functions, can enhance the competitiveness and the service level of a company, as discussed by Christopher (2011). According to Bolumole (2003), there exists an imbalance between what companies seek to achieve and what they are able to perform in-house. Therefore, "the rationale for outsourcing to third party increases" (Bolumole 2003, p.93).

This assignment will illustrate the development of third party logistics companies (3PLs) from the initial outsourcing to a collaborative partnership in supply chains today. The essay will be divided into three parts: development of 3PL, drivers for outsourcing as well as outsourced activities and how these add value to businesses.

Development of Third Party Logistics

Third party logistics, also known as outsourcing logistics activities (Grant et al. 2006; Bolumole 2003), has become more popular over the last four decades. According to Halldorsson and Skjøtt-Larsen (2004), there exists no consistent definition of a 3PL company nowadays and there is a variety of approaches in defining 3PL (Andersson 1997).

Historically, relationships with 3PLs were based on basic functions such as warehousing and transportation (Chopra and Meindl 2007). Each 3PL provider was a specialist in one part of a business (Persson and Virum 2001). Berglund et al. (1999) states three stages in the development of 3PL. In 1980, traditional logistics providers developed, who focused on transportation or warehousing. Both the deregulation of the transportation industry in the USA in 1980 and the following implementation of free-trade zones emphasized a trend towards globalization and a development of 3PL. Therefore, many transportation carrier installed modern systems for information and communication and were able to provide more efficient transport systems (Sheffi 1990). Thus, traditional logistics suppliers emerged to 3PLs to perform logistics activities for companies that were previously carried out in-house (Menon et al. 1998). The second stage in 1990 describes the entrance of network players like DHL, UPS and TNT into the market. This development, together with an increasing customer expectation, lead to the demand of integrated logistics services as the basic functions have become commoditized (Berglund et al. 1999). Therefore, carriers expanded their portfolio and began offering an overall set of integrated logistics activities (Chopra and Meindl 2007; Hertz and Alfredsson 2003). As discussed by Lynch (1998), the services offered in the USA by 3PLs expanded rapidly after the deregulation of the transportation industry and besides the initial transportation and warehousing, value-added services were adopted by 3PLs (cited in Andersson 1997). In this decade, 3PLs became very important in logistical management (Murphy and Poist 2000). In addition, all parties involved started to share necessary information to become more efficient and competitive (Christopher 2011). The last stage, as discussed by Berglund et al. (1999), began in the late 1990s, where players of financial services, management consultancy and information technology entered the market and are working together with participants from the other stages. Since the late 1990s the trend of outsourcing a wide range of supply chain activities has increased significantly (Chopra and Meindl 2007).

Therefore, today's provided logistics activities require more strategic expertise in contrast to the traditionally offered basic functions. The following definitions emphasize the development of 3PLs and their services offered to customers. Stefansson (2006, p.80) described 3PL services and relationships as follows:

> The third-party logistics arrangements cover straightforward arm's-length relationships involving everything from a few, rather simple logistics activities to advanced logistics solutions including value-added activities such as merge-in-transit setups.

According to Berglund et al. (1999) and Hertz and Alfredsson (2003) a 3PL provider can be defined as an external company who provides logistics services to a customer and acts as an intermediary between the supplier (1st party) and the customer (2nd party). The services offered can consist of, but are not limited to the traditional functions of transportation and warehousing. It can also include operational, strategic and tactical services such as information services, value-added services and the management of supply chains. The relationship can be seen as a long-term partnership as opposed to a distant contractual relationship. Especially when referring to long-term relationships between the involved parties, both benefit because the 3PL provider encompasses a large number of activities. In comparison with the definition of Stefansson (2006), this definition points out the length of the arrangement between the supplier and the 3PL provider. It emphasizes the change from historical, function-based outsourcing with a traditional arm's length relationship, to focus on mutual, closely integrated long-term relationships and the management of varying activities (Bolumole 2003; Hertz and Alfredsson 2003). Because of its strategic importance and value, 3PL is today closely related to the overall corporate strategy and therefore is part of many supply chain activities today.

Drivers for Outsourcing

The increasing competition in the global business environment and the importance of Supply Chain Management can be seen as reasons that have led many companies to focus on those functions in their supply chain where they can provide a competitive advantage (Zacharia et al. 2011; Christopher 2011). Therefore, McIvor (2009) recommends specializing only in core areas and outsourcing non-core activities, which were carried out previously within the business (Figure 1).

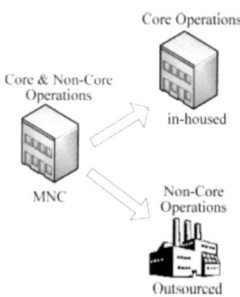

Figure 1: Business operations, competencies, and outsourcing
(extracted from Bansal et al. 2008,p.8302)

The decision to make or buy an activity, i.e. whether to outsource or to keep it in-house, is a core aspect of the business of 3PLs (Mentzer et al. 2007), because logistics management activities "are deemed as noncore functions for many firms" (Zacharia et al. 2011, p.40) and critical for most firms (Hobbs 1996). Mentzer et al. (2007) stated that companies whose core competency does not lie with logistics or certain components of logistics will consider outsourcing these operations to 3PLs, because they can execute them more effectively and efficiently. Le Bon and Hughes (2009) divide the reasons for outsourcing into three parts: saving of costs, improvement of service due to the expertise of contracted service providers and the focus on own core strengths. However, there are different and no clear views what the key drivers for outsourcing activities are.

Rushton et al. (2010) splits the mayor drivers for outsourcing into four categories: organizational, financial, service and physical. Organizational factors include the focus on the company's expertise whereas financial factors concentrate on capital cost advantages, i.e. companies do not have to invest anymore in warehouses and resources while using 3PLs. In addition, the service offered can be improved because 3PLs provide flexibility and a portfolio of value-added services. Both have a positive impact on the customer relationship. Physical factors describe the planning and management of widespread logistics activities due to the expertise of 3PLs. Moreover, many companies only use 3PLs on occasion, e.g. for peaks in demand, non-standard operations or promotion activities (Rushton et al. 2010). Eyefortransport (2005) carried out a survey in which they pointed out the key drivers for outsourcing (Figure 2).

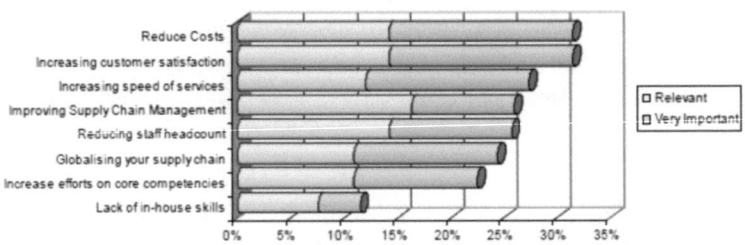

Figure 2: Drivers for outsourcing
(extracted from Eyefortransport 2005, p.5)

In addition, suppliers often decide to outsource their logistics services, because their supply chain management becomes too complex. Hence, many 3PLs support the supplier to resolve cultural incompatibility due to their comprehensive global expertise (Rushton et al. 2010). Moreover, companies outsource to benefit from the 3PLs wide network of logistics relationships and the efficiency provided (Zacharia et al. 2011).

However, Rushton et al. (2010) announced that the question whether to source an activity out to a 3PL provider or to carry it out in-house depends on several impacts, such as the industry, type of company and the products offered. Chopra and Meindl (2007) summarize "the decision to outsource is based on the growth in supply chain surplus provided by the third party and the increase in risk incurred by using a third party" (p.419).

Outsourced activities and how these add value to the business

The definitions in the first chapter have already provided some logistics activities that might be outsourced by a company. According to Bolumole (2003), firms usually outsource only some parts of the logistics function, i.e. especially operational functions, whereas strategic functions are still carried out in-house. Zacharia et al. (2011) differentiate between four scopes: outsourcing a specific task; a larger variety of functions; the design, implementation and management of particular complete functions as well as the adoption of the integral responsibility for certain activities. According to Sheffi (1990), there exists a large variety of activities which are offered by 3PLs. In a survey, conducted in 2013, interviewed persons stated that international transportation, domestic transportation and warehousing are the most frequently used services offered by 3PLs as shown in Figure 3 (The State of Logistics Outsourcing 2013).

Outsourced Logistics Service	Shipper Percentages				
	All Regions	North America	Europe	Asia-Pacific	Latin America
International Transportation	76%	64%	86%	79%	82%
Domestic Transportation	71	67	81	76	61
Warehousing	63	61	72	59	51
Freight Forwarding	53	54	60	46	47
Customs Brokerage	52	52	57	44	57
Reverse Logistics (defective, repair, return)	26	27	31	23	19
Cross-Docking	25	29	31	18	19
Product Labeling, Packaging, Assembly, Kitting	25	25	31	21	20
Transportation Planning and Management	22	24	27	19	15
Inventory Management	19	16	15	21	17
Freight Bill Auditing and Payment	18	32	13	11	5
Order Management and Fulfilment	16	20	18	16	9
Information Technology (IT) Services	13	16	16	14	9
Service Parts Logistics	12	11	14	12	12
Customer Service	10	8	7	17	14
Supply Chain Consultancy Services Provided by 3PLs	10	14	7	9	9
Fleet Management	8	8	8	8	9
LLP (Lead Logistics Provider) / 4PL Services	8	8	17	4	4
Sustainability/Green Supply Chain-Related Services	6	3	7	6	6

Figure 3: Activities outsourced to 3PL providers
(extracted from The State of Logistics Outsourcing 2013, p.10)

The figure emphasizes that the traditional functions of transportation and warehousing are the most common used activities of 3PLs. However, the service activities of 3PLs have extended during the last decades due to an increased demand (Power and Sharafali 2007). These additional activities are called value-added services, e.g. repacking, packaging, inbound logistics or e-fulfilment (Rushton et al. 2010). Many 3PLs are also able to provide administrative services, such as purchasing, forecasting and insurance and payment services (Stefansson 2006).

The mentioned drivers for outsourcing already provided some insights into how outsourcing might add value to businesses. The most important benefit of outsourcing activities to 3PLs can be seen in the increasing focus of a company in its core strengths. Companies outsource activities because they can be operated better by someone else (Persson and Virum 2001; Christopher 2011) or due to a lack of expertise in a process (Rushton et al. 2010). Furthermore, 3PLs provide updated information technology (Simchi-Levi et al. 2000). Due to modern systems and specialized expertise in logistics activities, a higher service level might be provided to the customer (Benson et al. 1994; Waters 2010). 3PLs provide a wider knowledge, i.e. they are well grounded in local knowledge and usually cover a wide geographical area, so that they are able to offer the best service to satisfy the requirements of a customer (Waters 2003). Moreover, this enhances the opportunities of operational improvements (Rushton et al. 2010). In addition, companies are able to improve their own liquidity and flexibility due to changing fixed costs into variable costs while outsourcing logistics activities. This effect results from the transferring of all included assets to 3PLs and a payment only for used services (Harrison and van Hoek 2005; Waters 2003). Furthermore, operating, labour and capital costs can be saved due to fewer investments in resources and facilities (Rushton et al. 2010). Especially, the outsourcing of logistics processes to 3PLs can minimize company's transaction costs, because of dealing with fewer relationships (Zacharia et al. 2011).

Berglund et al. (1999) state the existence of four ways adding value to the business of a customer. The first way is the competence of 3PLs "to achieve operational efficiency at a higher level" (p.66) in comparison with the level the customer himself would achieve. The key factor for adding value are the lower costs compared to those of a customer for e.g. running a warehouse efficiently. Another way of adding value is sharing resources between customers. 3PLs are able to add value due to economies of scale, because of having the possibility to e.g. share a warehouse among several customers (Berglund et al. 1999). This also effects a reduction of risks within the supply chain, because 3PLs have the possibility to share risks with many companies that are served by the logistics providers (Chopra and Meindl 2007). Moreover, by vertical or horizontal integration 3PLs can create a multi-purpose network, which enhances the value of an outsourced business and offers the customer an integral logistics solution. The last option of value creation emphasizes the use of specific logistics skills to manage, integrate and optimize the supply chain of a customer (Berglund et al. 1999).

Conclusion

The development of 3PLs from the initial outsourcing to their partnership in supply chain activities today has been analysed in this essay.

3PLs today play an integral part in Supply Chain Management. The changing competitive business environment has had a substantial impact on the development of the 3PLs. In today's economy where it is important to concentrate on core competencies, 3PLs have become an increasingly important part of future business success. However, despite of the importance and potential benefits of 3PLs, outsourcing brings with it a number of risks (Christopher 2011). The risk of lost control of the process, together with reduced customer contact and the leakage of sensitive data and information, are risks that companies must evaluate before moving functions to 3PLs (Chopra and Meindl 2007).

According to Christopher (2011), modern supply networks have become more global and complex due to the development of globalization. As supply chain thinking values the market, competition is not anymore "company against company but rather supply chain against supply chain" (p.15). Therefore, today exists the need for organisations that use their expertise of supply chains and specialist 3PLs to manage and integrate the entire supply chains. These organisations are named 4PL. With regards to this change in development, there is the necessity for many 3PLs for a continuous development, e.g. to become 4PL provider, to stay competitive in the global market.

List of references

Andersson, D. (1997) *Third Party Logistics – Outsourcing Logistics in Partnerships*, Linköping Studies in Management, Diss. No. 34

Bansal, M., Karimi, I. and Srinivasan, R. (2008) 'Selection of Third-Party Service Contracts for Chemical Logistics?', *Industrial & Engineering Chemistry Research*, 47, 8301-8316

Benson, D., Bugg, R. and Whitehead, G. (1994) *Transport and Logistics*, Hemel Hempstead: Woodhead-Faulkner (Publishers) Limited

Berglund, M., van Laarhoven, P., Sharman, G. and Wandel, S. (1999) 'Third-Party Logistics: Is There a Future?', *The International Journal of Logistics Management*, 10 (1), 59-70

Bolumole, Y. (2003) 'Evaluating the Supply Chain Role of Logistics Service Providers', *The International Journal of Logistics Management*, 14 (2), 93-104

Chopra, S. and Meindl, P. (2007) *Supply Chain Management Strategy, Planning & Operation*, 3rd ed., Harlow: Pearson Education Limited

Christopher, M. (2011) *Logistics and Supply Chain Management*, 4th ed., Harlow: Pearson Education Limited

Eyefortransport (2005) 'Outsourcing Logistics – The latest trends in using 3PL providers', [online], available:http://www.lomag-man.org/gestion%20stock_wms/englishversion_documents/ eyefortransportOutsourcing_3plLogistics2005Report.pdf [accessed 28 September, 2013]

Grant, D., Lambert, D., Stock, J. and Ellram, L. (2006) *Fundamentals of Logistics Management*, Maidenhead: McGraw-Hill Education

Halldorsson, A. and Skjøtt-Larsen, T. (2004) 'Developing logistics competencies through third party logistics relationships', *International Journal of Operations and Production Management*, 24 (2), 192 – 206

Harrison, A. and van Hoek, R. (2005) *Logistics Management and Strategy*, 2nd ed., Harlow: Pearson Education Limited

Hertz, S. and Alfredsson, M. (2003) 'Strategic development of third party logistics providers', *Industrial Marketing Management*, 32, 139-149

Hobbs, J. (1996) 'A Transaction Cost Approach to Supply Chain Management', *Supply Chain Management*, 1 (2), 15-27

Le Bon, J. and Hughes, D. (2009) 'The dilemma of outsourced customer service and care: Research propositions from a transaction cost perspective', *Industrial Marketing Management*, 38, 404-410

McIvor, R. (2009) 'How the transaction cost and resource-based theories of the firm inform outsourcing evaluation', *Journal of Operations Management*, 27, 45-63

Menon, M., McGinnis, M. and Ackerman, K. (1998) 'Selection criteria for providers of third-party logistics services: An exploratory story', *Journal of Business Logistics*, 19 (1), 121-137

Mentzer, J., Myers, M. and Stank, T. (2007) *Handbook of Global Supply Chain Management*, London: Sage Publications Limited

Murphy, P. and Poist, R. (2000) 'Third-party logistics: Some user versus provider perspectives', *Journal of Business Logistics*, 21 (1), 121-133

Persson, G. and Virum, H. (2001) 'Growth Strategies for Logistics Service Providers: A Case Study', *The International Journal of Logistics Management*, 12 (1), 53-64

Power, D. and Sharafali, M. (2007) 'Adding value through outsourcing: Contribution of 3PL services to customer performance', *Management Research News*, 30 (3), 228-235

Rushton, A., Croucher, P. and Baker, P. (2010) *The Handbook of Logistics & Distribution Management*, 4th ed., London: Kogan Page Limited

Sheffi, Y. (1990) 'Third Party Logistics: Present and Future Prospects', *Journal of Business Logistics*, 11 (2), 27-39

Simchi-Levi, D., Kaminsky, P. and Simchi-Levi, E. (2000) *Designing and Managing the Supply Chain,* United States of America: McGraw-Hill Higher Education

Stefansson, G. (2006) 'Collaborative logistics management and the role of third-party service providers', *International Journal of Physical Distribution & Logistics Management,* 36 (2), 76-92

The State of Logistics Outsourcing (2013) '2013 Third-Party Logistics – results and findings of the 17th annual study', [online], available: http://www.panalpina.com/content/www/global/de/home/ news_media/publications/3pl-study/_jcr_content/contentParSys/download/downloadList/ german.spooler.download/2013%203PL%20Study.pdf [accessed 29 September, 2013]

Waters, D. (2010) *Global Logistics New Directions in Supply Chain Management,* 6th ed., London: Kogan Page Limited

Waters, D. (2003) *Inventory Control and Management,* 2nd ed., Chichester: John Wiley & Sons Limited

Zacharia, Z., Sanders, N. and Nix, N. (2011) 'The Emerging Role of the Third-Party Logistics Provider (3PL) as an Orchestrator', *Journal of Business Logistics,* 32 (1), 40-54